To hear
the whale

song,

turn to the
last page of this
book and pull
out the tab!

Whales

by Michele Babineau McNeill

SCHOLASTIC INC.

New York   Toronto   London   Auckland   Sydney
Mexico City   New Delhi   Hong Kong   Buenos Aires

ISBN 0-545-08465-2

Text and illustrations copyright © 2008 by Scholastic Inc.

Printed in China
First printing, November 2008

Photo Credits

Cover: Seapics; Back cover: Joyce Photographics/Photo Researchers Inc.;
pg.4–5: F.Stuart Westmorland/Photo Researchers Inc. Paul A. Souders/Corbis;
pg. 6: Francois Gohier/Photo Researchers Inc.; pg. 7: Seapics; pp 2 and 8: Seapics;
pg . 8: Joyce Photographics/Photo Researchers Inc., Richard Ellis/Photo Researchers Inc.; pg 9: Seapics, Francois Gohier/Photo Researchers Inc.; pg 10–11: Gordon Langsbury/Bruce Coleman Inc.; pg. 12–13: Richard Ellis/Photo Researchers Inc.;
pg. 14–15: Flip Nicklin/Minden Pictures; pg.17: Flip Nicklin/Minden Pictures;
pg. 18: Paul Souders/Corbis; pg.19: Francois Gohier/Photo Researchers, Brandon Cole;
pg 21: Vanias/Shutterstock; pg 22: Seapics, Philip Lange/Shutterstock, AFP Photo/Andy Newman; pp. 1 and 24: Flip Nicklin/Minden Pictures; pg.25: Seapics; pg 27: Kelly-Mooney Photography/Corbis, Museum of History and Industry/Corbis;
pg 29: Bud Lehnhausen/Photo Researchers,Inc.

Contents

CHAPTER 1

Whales Are Special

Whales are special animals. They are the largest animals in the world. Some are even bigger than the dinosaurs were! Even though whales spend their whole lives in the water, they aren't fish.

Bottlenose Dolphin ▶

FAST FACT
Dolphins are part of the whale family.

Whales are mammals, just like you and me. They spend time together in pods, which are like whale families. Whales are also very smart and can communicate with each other through sound. Some whales even sing!

Whales have a lot in common with you and me. They have lungs and breathe air. Since whales live in the ocean, they have to rise to the surface of the water to breathe. They take a deep breath before they dive to eat. When they come to the surface again, they exhale, and the force of their breath shoots a spray of mist through their blowholes. Like us, whales are warm blooded. Warm-blooded mammals are able to keep the inside of their bodies at the same warm termperature no matter how cold or hot it is outside. Whales also give birth to live young and nurse their young with milk. These baby whales, called calves, even have hair!

▲ Blue Whale

Whales breathe through a blowhole, which is like a nostril.

Whales are social animals, and some whales live in groups called pods. Whales in a pod will hunt, migrate and even raise their young together. A pod can include up to 100 whales or as few as two or three whales. The strongest social bond is between a mother and her baby, or calf. Female whales, called cows, protect their calves for an extended period of time, often as long as a year.

▲ Humpback Whale mother and calf

Baby whales grow at an amazing rate. They gain almost 10 pounds an hour! That's a ton every nine days!

CHAPTER 2
Types of Whales

There are two types of whales: toothed whales and baleen whales. **Toothed whales** hunt for **prey**. They grab smaller sea creatures like fish and seals with their teeth and eat them whole. The number of teeth in a toothed whale can range from one, like the narwhal, to as many as 100 in some dolphins. The killer whale, or orca, is a toothed whale. The sperm whale and beluga whale are also toothed whales.

Narwhals use their tusks in a show of strength like medieval knights jousting.

Whale teeth curve backwards to help whales catch and hold their prey.

▼ Southern Right Whale

Baleen is lined with hair-like plates,
as seen here.

Baleen whales do not have teeth. When baleen whales eat, they gulp huge amounts of water or mud. Then, they use a comb-like structure, called a **baleen**, to filter out tiny **crustaceans** and small fish from the water to eat. Baleen whales are usually much bigger than toothed whales. The blue, humpback, gray whale and right whale are all examples of baleen whales.

FAST FACT
Baleen is made of **keratin**, the same material fingernails are made of.

9

TOOTHED WHALES

Fluke
Toothed whales use their fins and tail **fluke** to race after prey.

Dorsal Fin

The killer whale, also called an orca whale, is a toothed whale. Despite its name, the killer whale does not harm people.

Teeth
Toothed whales hunt for prey and catch food with their teeth.

Blowhole
Toothed whales have one blowhole.

Ears
Toothed whales use their keen hearing to hunt. Whales' ears are tiny, thin tubes inside their head.

11

BALEEN WHALES

Blowholes
Baleen whales have 2 blowholes.

Throat Pleats
Baleen whales have throat grooves that expand to hold huge amounts of water.

Baleen
Baleen strains food from the water like a giant filter.

RICHARD ELLIS~1974

Dorsal Fin

Fluke

The blue whale is a baleen whale. Blue whales are the largest creatures on Earth.

CHAPTER 3

Whale Song

Whales can make a lot of noise. They squeak, click, groan and moan. Toothed whales use sound to help them navigate in the large ocean and find prey. This is called **echolocation**. They send out sounds that bounce back from nearby objects and tell them how large and how far away those objects are. Whales also use sound to communicate their location to other whales.

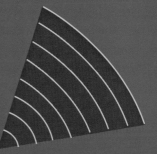

▲ Humpback Whale

Whale songs are another way whales communicate with each other. Different kinds of whales sing different kinds of songs. Scientists aren't sure what the songs mean, or even how the whales make sound, since whales don't have vocal cords. Singing whales may be protecting their territory or trying to attract a mate. Songs include a repeated pattern of certain sounds, such as groans or moans or chirps. This pattern is called a phrase. A group of consecutive phrases make up a theme. A group of predictable themes make up a song.

FAST FACT

Humpback whale songs can last for 20 minutes and can be heard hundreds of miles away!

Scientists study whale songs to learn about the language of these amazing creatures.

YOU CAN LISTEN

to the humpback whale song in this book!

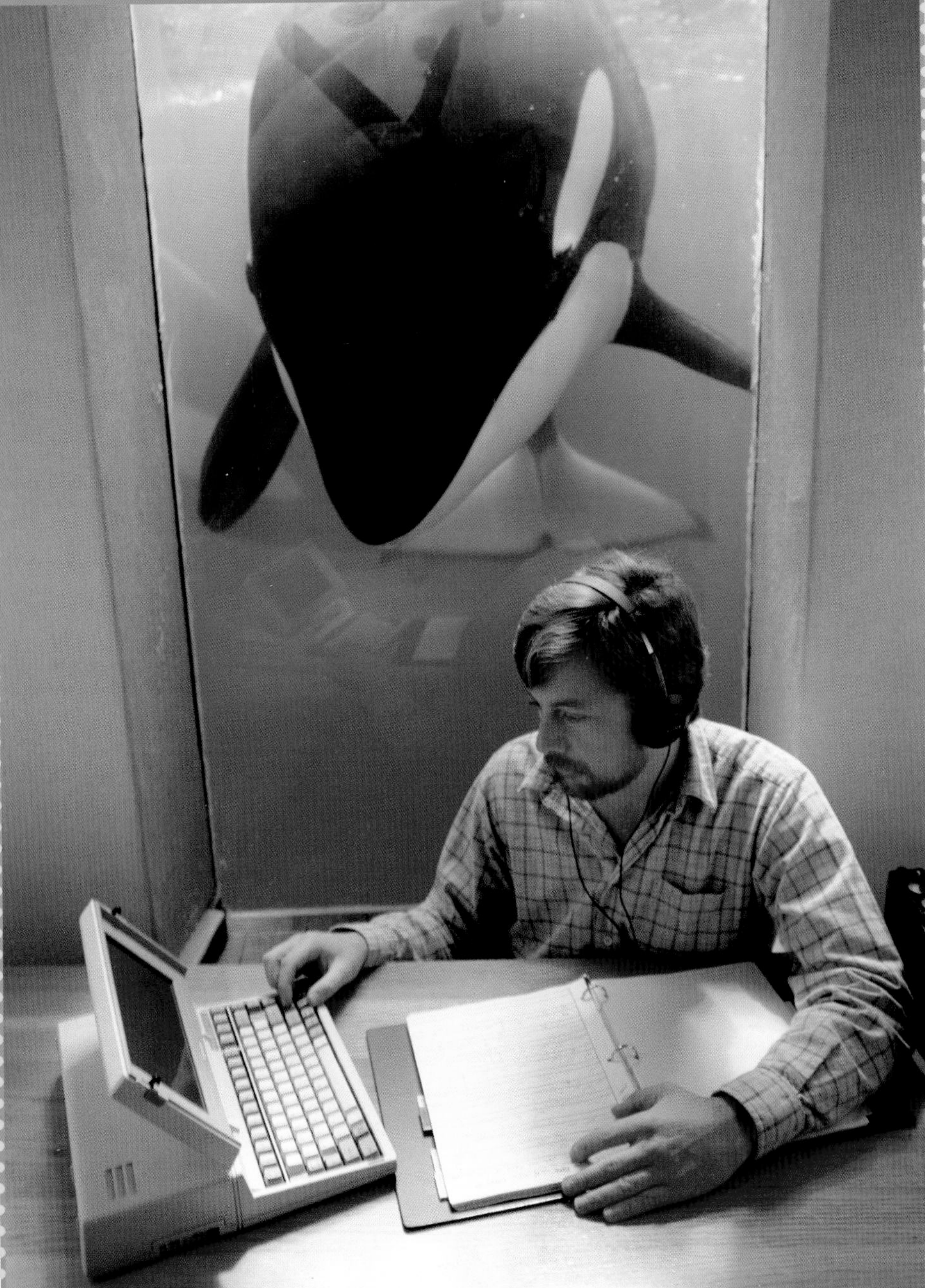

CHAPTER 4

Whale Behavior

Because whales spend so much time underwater where we can't see them, their behavior above the water is what we see most. The three most common whale behaviors are **breaching**, **lobtailing**, and **spyhopping**.

Breaching is when a whale propels its body up and out of the water and then lands with a loud slam and a big splash. No one is sure why whales breach, but it may be to communicate their location to other whales, or to dislodge barnacles from their skin, or maybe just because it's fun!

When a whale lobtails, it picks up its tail and slaps it loudly on the water. This is a way to communicate location or to assert dominance.

Spyhopping is when a whale comes up vertically out of the water and looks around. The whale may be looking for prey, for members of its pod, or at a whale-watching boat that happens to be nearby!

CHAPTER 5
Migration

Many whales travel long distances each year. This is called **migration**. Migrations usually happen in the spring and fall. Many baleen whales and some of the toothed whales migrate.

In the summer, whales travel to eat. In the winter, they travel to breed. The food that most whales eat, krill, is most abundant in cold waters. But when it is time for the cows to birth their calves, the whales move to warmer, shallow water. Shallow water is safer for calves.

When whales are born, they can not swim, and need their mothers to guide them to the surface so they can breathe. There are also fewer predators in the shallow water.

Grey whales migrate from the Arctic Ocean to the Baja peninsula off Mexico and back. That's more than 11,000 miles roundtrip! (18,000kms)

Some beluga whales travel from the deep cold of the Arctic Ocean to warmer coastal waters to breed. Humpback whales winter in the Gulf of Maine and summer in the Caribbean.

CHAPTER 6

Record Breakers

BIGGEST WHALE

The adult female blue whale is the biggest animal on the planet and can grow to be more than 100 feet long. That is about the size of a Boeing 737 airplane! The blue whale's tail fluke is as wide as a soccer goal.

A blue whale is 3 times the size of a school bus.

smallest whale

The dwarf sperm whale is the smallest whale. An adult dwarf sperm whale is only 7 to 9 feet long, which is smaller than some dolphins.

23

Fastest Whale

The fastest whale is the killer whale. A male killer whale, called a **bull,** can reach speeds up to 30 miles per hour! Killer whales will swim quickly in order to catch their prey. Killer whales are the largest member of the dolphin family.

Killer whales are no threat to humans, but they are the deadliest predators in the ocean. When they hunt in groups, they can kill much larger creatures, including other whales.

Sperm whales are the deepest divers. They dive to catch their favorite food, which is giant squid. Giant squid live on the ocean floor. Sperm whales regularly dive 4,000 feet to feed, and can hold their breath for up to 2 hours!

FAST FACT

The sperm whale has the biggest brain of any animal! It can weigh 20 pounds!

CHAPTER 7
whales in Danger

Hunting for whales is called **whaling**. Starting in the 16th century, whales were hunted for their meat and **blubber**, which was melted and used as fuel and as cooking oil. Whale parts were also used to make cosmetics and soap. Baleen was used in clothing.

Whale hunters in North America.

Whale teeth were used in the art of scrimshaw and baleen plates were used in a variety of items, including corsets and fishing rods.

Whaling became so popular that some whales were in danger of becoming extinct. In 1946, the International Whaling Commission was created to keep the whale population from disappearing. Countries that joined the group agreed to laws against hunting whales that are in danger of becoming **extinct**. Countries that are not members of the IWC still hunt whales.

Some whales are also hurt by collisions with ships or when they are trapped in fishing gear. Others are endangered because the oceans they live in are becoming polluted.

What can be done?

What can you do to help? Learning more about whales is good place to start! There are many whale watching tours around the world. There are also Adopt-A-Whale programs that help fund research and protection programs for whales. These efforts help the whale population remain healthy and strong. You can also write letters to your state legislators asking them to support laws against whaling.

FAST FACT

Humpback whales have been a protected species since 1963.

Blue whales being observed by whale watchers in Baja, California.

Glossary

baleen: Comb-like plates that hang from the jaw of baleen whales and are used to strain food from the ocean

blowhole: An opening on the top of a whale's head used for breathing

blow: The spray of moisture and air when a whale exhales

blubber: The layer of fat underneath a whale's skin

breaching: Leaping out of the water

bull: An adult male whale

calf: A baby whale

cow: An adult female whale

crustaceans: Small sea creatures with shells, including shrimp and crabs

echolocation: System to locate prey and other objects in the ocean by using sound

extinct: Describes a type of animal that has died out and no longer exists

fluke: A whale's tail

keratin: The protein that makes up baleen

lobtailing: Raising the tail and slamming it down on the water's surface

mammals: Animals that have hair, are warm-blooded, and nurse their young

migration: Moving from one area to another in search of food and breeding grounds

pod: A group of whales traveling together

prey: An animal hunted by another animal for food

spyhopping: Sticking the head out of the water in order to look around

throat pleats: Pleats on a baleen whale that expand when it gulps large amounts of water

toothed whales: Whales with teeth

whaling: Hunting for whales

31

Index